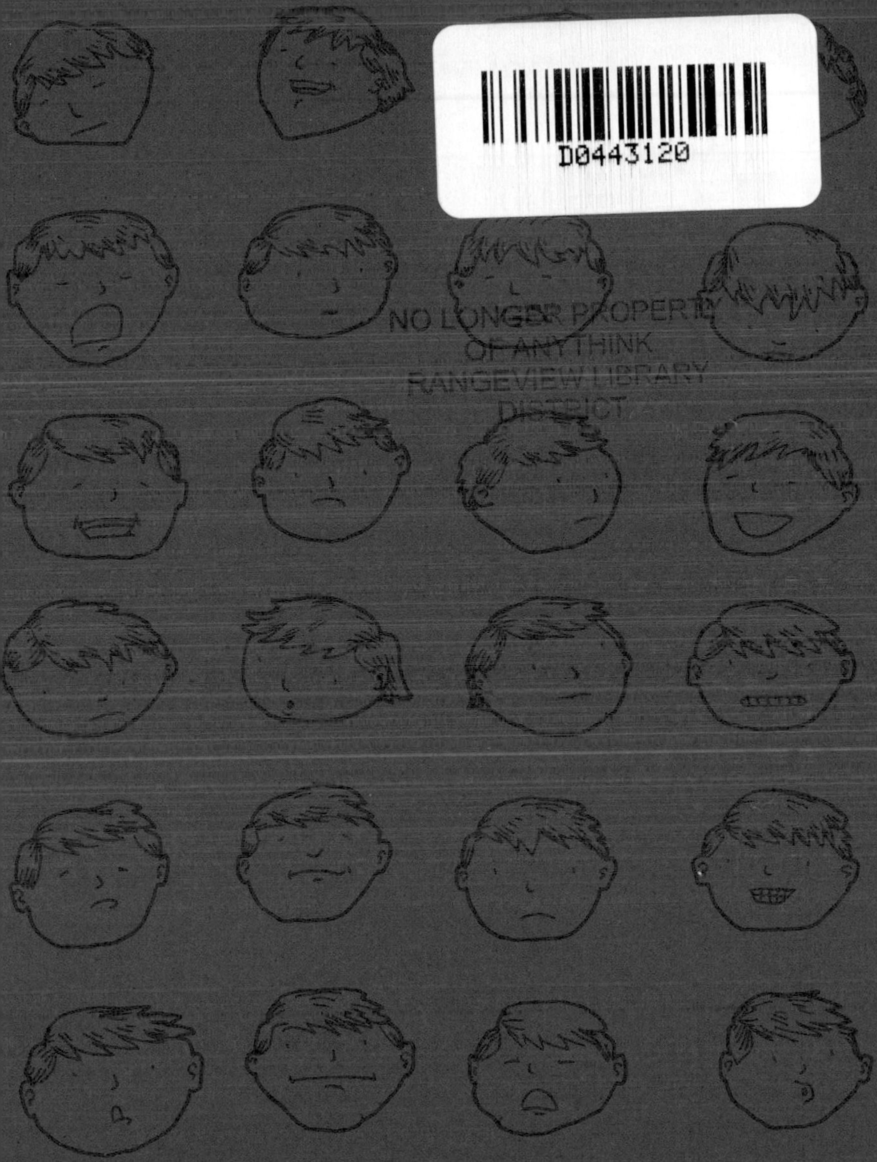

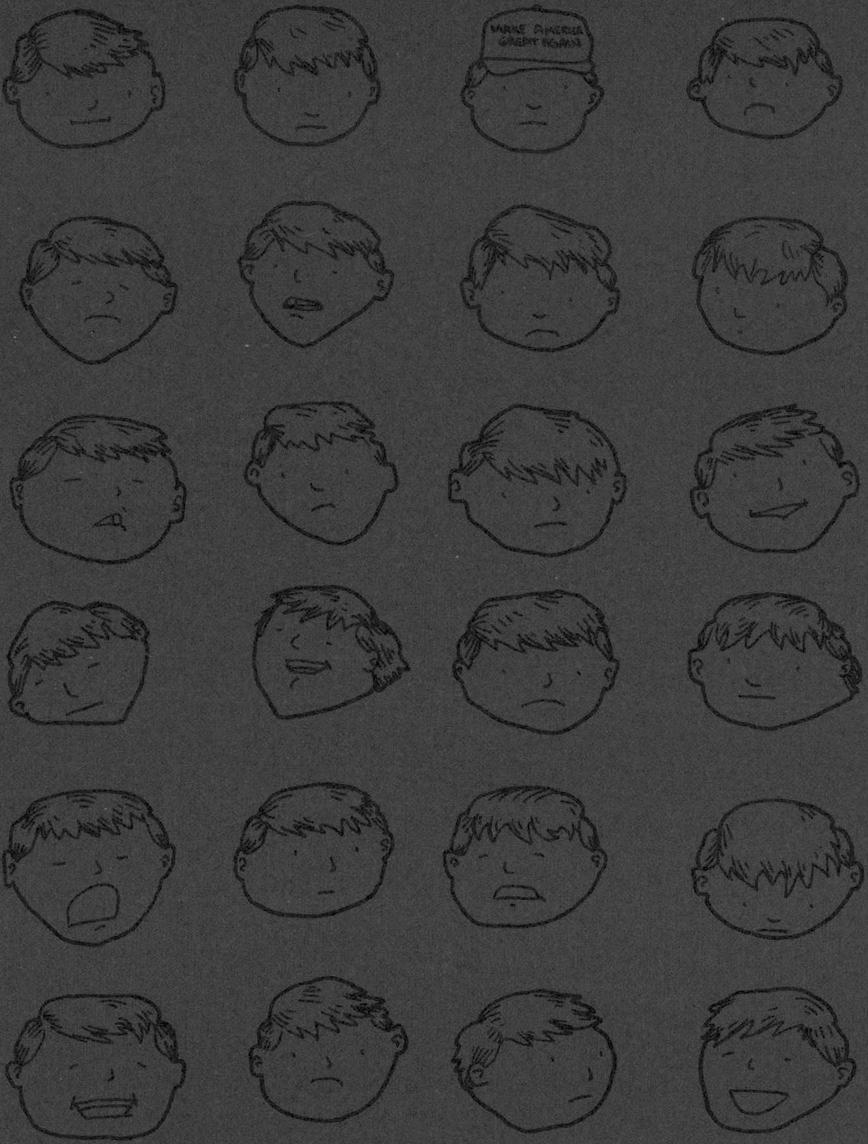
MAKE AMERICA GREAT AGAIN

SH*T
MY
PRESIDENT
SAYS

SHANNON
WHEELER

SH*T MY PRESIDENT SAYS

The Illustrated Tweets of
Donald J. Trump

by @MuchCoffee

Also by Shannon Wheeler:

Too Much Coffee Man
How to Be Happy
I Thought You Would Be Funnier
Children with Glue

With Mark Russell:

God Is Disappointed in You
Apocrypha Now

*Sh*t My President Says*
© 2017 Shannon Wheeler

Published by
Top Shelf Productions
PO Box 1282
Marietta, GA 30061-1282
USA

Editor-in-Chief: Chris Staros

Visit our online catalog at
www.topshelfcomix.com.

Printed in Korea.

21 20 19 18 17   1 2 3 4 5

Edited by Chris Staros, Greg Goldstein,
and Leigh Walton.
Designed by Eric Skillman.

FOREWORD BY BOB MANKOFF

 Bob Mankoff @BobMankoff
Cartoon and Humor Editor, *Esquire* Magazine

Trump packs a lot into his 140 character tweets. Wheeler's illustrations unpack them.

INTRODUCTION BY SHANNON WHEELER

I read over 30,000 of Donald (@realDonaldTrump) Trump's
tweets. My bad dreams started around the 10,000th tweet. I'll
skip the details, but I've lost my taste for pudding and British
medical dramas.

Most of Trump's tweets are promotional: he links to articles
about himself, he quotes his own books, he loves interviews,
and he encourages you to stay in his hotels and play on his
golf courses. But a number of his tweets are personal and
appear unfiltered. Through this round-the-clock stream of
consciousness, he expresses his desires, fears, and petty
obsessions, his real personality.

His implicit message isn't about himself, it's about his reader. He
encourages his fans to be themselves—not with aspiration, but
indulgence. Be sexist. Be racist. Be fearful. Be selfish. Hate and
fear the world. Consume. Be materialistic. Drive a big car. Drive
as much as you want—there's plenty of oil in the world. There's
enough for you. If we run out, Trump will do what it takes to
keep the oil flowing and the gas cheap. Enjoy yourself—Trump
will be the global bully to make sure our empire, and your self-
indulgence, is assured.

I'm not only looking to caricature and parody Trump; I also want to
understand his perspective and how it resonates with his supporters.
Using his own words, I want to show how he contradicts himself,
and lead the reader to question reality. I don't draw him as an ogre.
I draw him as a child—a petulant, misunderstood, self-absorbed,
self-righteous, narcissistic, spoiled brat of a child. Sometimes
hilarious, other times infuriating. By using Trump's own words, and
placing them in the context of his cartoon universe, I hope to give
the reader a better chance of understanding the mind we elected.
Like it or not, we can't ignore him.

Trump's first tweet was on the May 4th, 2009, to promote his appearance on the David Letterman show.

TRUMP TIMELINE

1946   Trump is born.

1971   Trump becomes president of his father's company.

1987   Trump considers a run for president.

2000   Trump briefly runs as a Reform Party candidate, then withdraws, but still wins two state primaries.

2003   Trump again considers running for president.

2004   *The Apprentice* premieres.

2009   @RealDonaldTrump tweets for the first time.

2011   Trump officially announces that he will not run for president.

2013   Trump forms a presidential exploratory committee.

2015   Trump leaves *The Apprentice*, then announces his candidacy for president.

2016   Trump wins the Republican nomination, then the general election.

2017   Trump enters the White House.

 **Donald J. Trump** ✔
@realDonaldTrump

Be sure to tune in and watch Donald Trump on Late
Night with David Letterman as he presents the Top Ten
List tonight!

May 4, 2009 2:54 PM

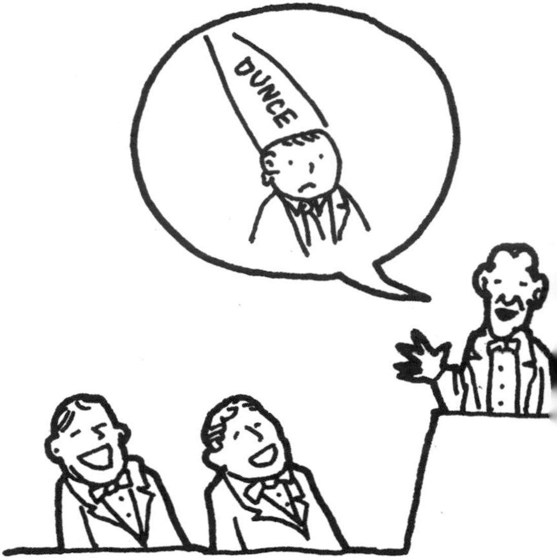
DUNCE

WHITE HOUSE CORRESPONDENTS' DINNER
MAY 1, 2011

 Donald J. Trump ✔
@realDonaldTrump

Isn't it crazy that people of little or no talent
or success can be so critical of those whose
accomplishments are great with no retribution

Jul 18, 2013 8:19 AM

 Donald J. Trump ✔
@realDonaldTrump

An 'extremely credible source' has called my office and told me that @BarackObama's birth certificate is a fraud.

Aug 6, 2012 4:23 PM

Donald J. Trump ✓
@realDonaldTrump

Letterman @Late_Show begging me to go back on his low rated show--calls lots--must apologize for racist comment.

Aug 30, 2012 3:32 PM

 Donald J. Trump ✔
@realDonaldTrump

.@DavidLetterman @Late_Show fully apologized last night for calling me a racist. Thank you David--we are again friends.

Oct 10, 2012 9:28 AM

Donald J. Trump ✔
@realDonaldTrump

Nobody wants wind turbines, they are failing all over the world and need massive subsidy--a disaster for taxpayers.

Aug 15, 2012 10:09 AM

 Donald J. Trump ✔
@realDonaldTrump

If Obama keeps pushing wind turbines our country will go down the tubes economically, environmentally & aesthetically.

Oct 17, 2012 11:53 AM

 Donald J. Trump ✔
@realDonaldTrump

Wind turbines are totally destroying the areas in which they are located--all for unreliable, bad & expensive energy!

Nov 27, 2012 11:15 AM

 Donald J. Trump ✔
@realDonaldTrump

In three years people won't be building wind turbines anymore - they are obsolete & totally destroy the environment in which they sit.

Apr 23, 2013 3:19 PM

 Donald J. Trump ✔
@realDonaldTrump

Wind turbines are a scourge to communities and
wildlife. They are environmental disasters.

Aug 23, 2012 2:09 PM

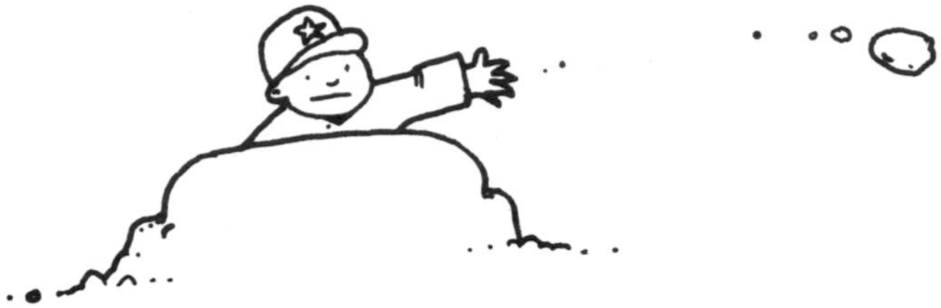

 Donald J. Trump ✔
@realDonaldTrump

The concept of global warming was created by and for
the Chinese in order to make U.S. manufacturing non-
competitive.

Nov 6, 2012 2:15 PM

 Donald J. Trump ✔
@realDonaldTrump

When someone attacks me, I always attack back...
except 100x more. This has nothing to do with a tirade
but rather, a way of life!

Nov 11, 2012 8:56 AM

 Donald J. Trump ✔
@realDonaldTrump

It makes me feel so good to hit "sleazebags" back --
much better than seeing a psychiatrist (which I
never have!)

Nov 19, 2012 11:06 AM

Donald J. Trump ✔
@realDonaldTrump

Robert Pattinson should not take back Kristen Stewart.
She cheated on him like a dog & will do it again--just watch.
He can do much better!

Oct 17, 2012 2:47 AM

Donald J. Trump ✔
@realDonaldTrump

Lots of response to my Pattinson/Kristen Stewart reunion.
She will cheat again--100 certain--am I ever wrong?

Oct 18, 2012 10:27 AM

Donald J. Trump ✔
@realDonaldTrump

Robert I'm getting a lot of heat for saying you should
dump Kristen- but I'm right. If you saw the Miss Universe
girls you would reconsider.

Oct 18, 2012 12:21 AM

Donald J. Trump ✔
@realDonaldTrump

Everyone knows I am right that Robert Pattinson
should dump Kristen Stewart. In a couple of years, he
will thank me. Be smart, Robert.

Oct 22, 2012 4:48 PM

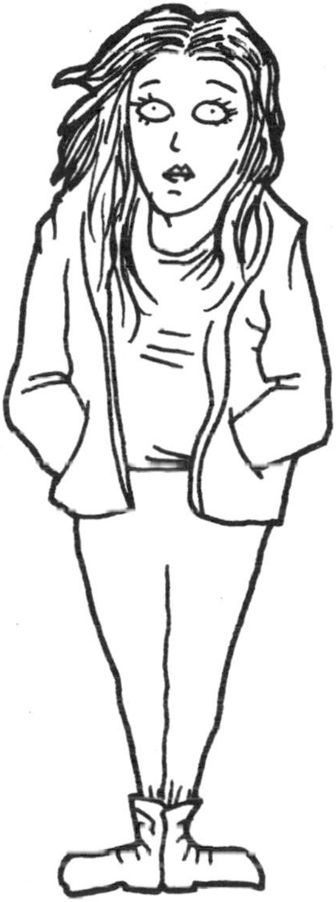

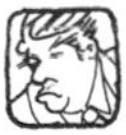

Donald J. Trump
@realDonaldTrump

"Donald Trump Wishes Kristen Stewart A Happy Birthday" http://t.co/UMN4QpgmHN via @HollywoodLife

Apr 10, 2013 3:06 PM

 Donald J. Trump ✔
@realDonaldTrump

I went to Wharton, made over $8 billion, employ
thousands of people & get insulted by morons who
can't get enough of me on twitter...!

Feb 12, 2013 4:34 PM

 Donald J. Trump ✔
@realDonaldTrump

Many people have commented that my fragrance,
"Success" is the best scent & lasts the longest. Try it
& let me know what you think!

Feb 27 , 2013 11:06 AM

 **Donald J. Trump** ✔
@realDonaldTrump

`@ForeverMcln: @realDonaldTrump how much would it take for you to make out with Rosie O'Donnell?" One trillion, at least!

Mar 2, 2013 12:11 AM

 Donald J. Trump ✔
@realDonaldTrump

Amazing how the haters & losers keep tweeting the
name "F**kface Von Clownstick" like they are so original
& like no one else is doing it...

May 3, 2013 12:35 PM

 Donald J. Trump ✽
@realDonaldTrump

Sorry losers and haters, but my I.Q. is one of the
highest -and you all know it! Please don't feel so stupid
or insecure,it's not your fault

May 8, 2013 9:37 PM

 **Donald J. Trump** ✔
@realDonaldTrump

It's freezing outside, where the hell is "global warming"??

May 25, 2013 7:00 PM

 **Donald J. Trump** ✔
@realDonaldTrump

Do you think Putin will be going to The Miss Universe
Pageant in November in Moscow - if so, will he become
my new best friend?

Jun 18, 2013 11:17 PM

 **Donald J. Trump** ✓
@realDonaldTrump

I would like to extend my best wishes to all, even the haters and losers, on this special date, September 11th.

Sep 11, 2013 7:21 AM

Donald J. Trump ✔
@realDonaldTrump

President Obama played golf yesterday???

Nov 18, 2013 7:59 AM

 **Donald J. Trump** ✔
@realDonaldTrump

Can you believe we still have not gotten our Marine out of Mexico. He sits in prison while our PRESIDENT plays golf and makes bad decisions!

Sep 26, 2014 6:35 PM

 Donald J. Trump ✔
@realDonaldTrump

Can you believe that,with all of the problems and difficulties facing the U.S., President Obama spent the day playing golf. Worse than Carter

Oct 13, 2014 8:03 PM

 Donald J. Trump ✔
@realDonaldTrump

We pay for Obama's travel so he can fundraise millions so Democrats can run on lies. Then we pay for his golf.

Oct 14, 2014 3:35 PM

Donald J. Trump ✔
@realDonaldTrump

President Obama has a major meeting on the N.Y.C.
Ebola outbreak, with people flying in from all over the
country, but decided to play golf!

Oct 23, 2014 11:54 PM

 **Donald J. Trump** ✔
@realDonaldTrump

Played golf today with Prime Minister Abe of Japan and
@TheBig_Easy, Ernie Els, and had a great time. Japan is
very well represented!

Feb 11, 2017 6:15 PM

 Donald J. Trump ✔
@realDonaldTrump

How amazing, the State Health Director who verified
copies of Obama's "birth certificate" died in plane crash
today. All others lived

Dec 12, 2013 4:32 PM

 Donald J. Trump ✔
@realDonaldTrump

Isn't it crazy, I'm worth billions of dollars, employ
thousands of people, and get libeled by moron bloggers
who can't afford a suit! WILD.

Feb 19, 2014 8:14 AM

Donald J. Trump ✔
@realDonaldTrump

I don't hate Obama at all, I just think he is an absolutely
terrible president, maybe the worst in our history!

Mar 20, 2014 8:10 PM

Donald J. Trump ✔
@realDonaldTrump

Healthy young child goes to the doctor, gets pumped
with massive vaccines, doesn't feel good and changes -
AUTISM. Many such cases!

Mar 28, 2014 8:35 AM

 **Donald J. Trump** ✔
@realDonaldTrump

Are you allowed to impeach a president for gross incompetence?

Jun 4, 2014 6:23 AM

 Donald J. Trump ✔
 @realDonaldTrump

How is ABC Television allowed to have a show entitled
"Blackish"? Can you imagine the furor of a show,
"Whiteish"! Racism at highest level?

Oct 1, 2014 8:41 AM

 **Donald J. Trump** ✓
@realDonaldTrump

Something very important, and indeed society changing,
may come out of the Ebola epidemic that will be a very
good thing: NO SHAKING HANDS!

Oct 4, 2014 1:14 AM

 Donald J. Trump ✔
@realDonaldTrump

President Obama - close down the flights from Ebola infected areas right now, before it is too late! What the hell is wrong with you?

Oct 4, 2014 8:05 PM

 **Donald J. Trump** ✔
@realDonaldTrump

Who is paying for that tedious Smokey Bear
commercial that is on all the time - enough already!

Jan 8, 2015 1:50 AM

 **Donald J. Trump** ✔
@realDonaldTrump

Record low temperatures and massive amounts of snow. Where the hell is GLOBAL WARMING?

Feb 14, 2015 11:23 PM

 **Donald J. Trump** ✔
@realDonaldTrump

The Oscars are a sad joke, very much like our
President. So many things are wrong!

Feb 23, 2015 12:26 AM

 **Donald J. Trump** ✔
@realDonaldTrump

If elected, I will undo all of Obama's executive orders.
I will deliver. Let's Make America Great Again!
donaldjtrump.com

May 4, 2015 3:09 PM

 Donald J. Trump ✔
@realDonaldTrump

When somebody challenges you unfairly, fight back - be brutal, be tough - don't take it. It is always important to WIN!

Jun 27, 2015 10:50 AM

 **Donald J. Trump** ✔
@realDonaldTrump

Legal immigrants want border security. It is common
sense. We must build a wall! Let's Make America Great
Again! pic.twitter.com/I5CybmR0MF

Jul 11, 2015 3:06 PM

 Donald J. Trump ✔
@realDonaldTrump

Had a special visitor in my office yesterday for @TIME photo shoot. pic.twitter.com/GoloYLeRZz

Aug 20, 2015 11:06 AM

Donald J. Trump ✔
@realDonaldTrump

Am I morally obligated to defend the president every time somebody says something bad or controversial about him? I don't think so!

Sep 19, 2015 8:45 AM

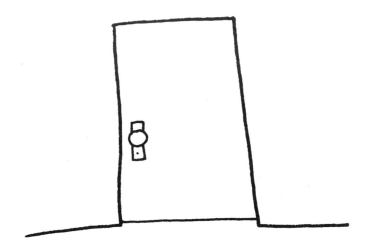

 **Donald J. Trump** ✔
@realDonaldTrump

Signing my tax return.... pic.twitter.com/XJfXeaORbU

Oct 15, 2015 1:13 PM

Donald J. Trump ✔
@realDonaldTrump

I LIVE IN NEW JERSEY & @realDonaldTrump IS RIGHT:
MUSLIMS DID CELEBRATE ON 9/11 HERE! WE SAW IT!
infowars.com/i-live-in-jers...

Nov 25, 2015 7:22 PM

 Donald J. Trump ✔
@realDonaldTrump

I do not know the reporter for the @nytimes, or what he looks like. I was showing a person groveling to take back a statement made long ago!

Nov 26, 2015 4:40 PM

 **Donald J. Trump** ✔
@realDonaldTrump

Meryl Streep, one of the most over-rated actresses in Hollywood, doesn't know me but attacked last night at the Golden Globes. She is a......

Jan 9, 2017 6:27 AM

 Donald J. Trump ✔
@realDonaldTrump

Hillary flunky who lost big. For the 100th time, I never "mocked" a disabled reporter (would never do that) but simply showed him.......

Jan 9, 2017 6:36 AM

 Donald J. Trump ✔
@realDonaldTrump

"groveling" when he totally changed a 16 year old story that he had written in order to make me look bad. Just more very dishonest media!

Jan 9, 2017 6:43 AM

 **Donald J. Trump** ✓
@realDonaldTrump

"@derektheeight: Will be interesting to see how many times Jersey rooftop will be brought up now that video has miraculously been found..."

Dec 3, 2015 8:12 AM

Donald J. Trump ✓
@realDonaldTrump

Obama said in his speech that Muslims are our sports heroes. What sport is he talking about, and who? Is Obama profiling?

Dec 7, 2015 12:50 AM

 **Donald J. Trump** ✔
@realDonaldTrump

We will stop heroin and other drugs from coming into
New Hampshire from our open southern border. We will
build a WALL and have security.

Feb 9, 2016 5:19 PM

 Donald J. Trump ✔
@realDonaldTrump

The phony lawsuit against Trump U could have been easily settled by me but I want to go to court. 98% approval rating by students. Easy win

Mar 3, 2016 9:21 AM

Donald J. Trump ✔
@realDonaldTrump

We must build a great wall between Mexico and the
United States! dailymail.co.uk/news/article-3...

Apr 1, 2016 5:49 PM

 Donald J. Trump ✔
@realDonaldTrump

While our wonderful president was out playing golf all
day, the TSA is falling apart, just like our government!
Airports a total disaster!

May 21, 2016 6:56 AM

Donald J. Trump ✓
@realDonaldTrump

Crooked Hillary wants to get rid of all guns and yet she is surrounded by bodyguards who are fully armed. No more guns to protect Hillary!

May 21, 2016 8:49 AM

 Donald J. Trump ✓
 @realDonaldTrump

I should have easily won the Trump University case on summary judgement but have a judge, Gonzalo Curiel, who is totally biased against me.

May 30, 2016 5:55 PM

Donald J. Trump ✔
@realDonaldTrump

Thank you to the LGBT community! I will fight for you
while Hillary brings in more people that will threaten
your freedoms and beliefs.

Jun 14, 2016 1:31 PM

 Donald J. Trump ✓
@realDonaldTrump

Mexico will pay for the wall!

Sep 1, 2016 6:31 AM

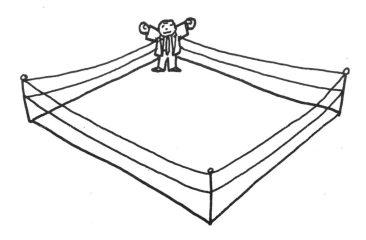

 **Donald J. Trump** ✔
@realDonaldTrump

It is so nice that the shackles have been taken off me
and I can now fight for America the way I want to.

Oct 11, 2016 10:00 AM

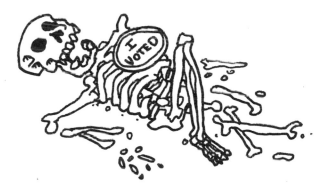

 **Donald J. Trump** ✔
@realDonaldTrump

TODAY WE MAKE AMERICA GREAT AGAIN!

Nov 8, 2016 6:43 AM

Donald J. Trump ✔
@realDonaldTrump

I settled the Trump University lawsuit for a small fraction of the potential award because as President I have to focus on our country.

Nov 19, 2016 8:34 AM

 Donald J. Trump ✓
@realDonaldTrump

In addition to winning the Electoral College in a landslide,
I won the popular vote if you deduct the millions of
people who voted illegally.

Nov 27 , 2016 3:30 PM

  **Donald J. Trump** ✓
@realDonaldTrump

The United States must greatly strengthen and expand
its nuclear capability until such time as the world comes
to its senses regarding nukes

Dec 22, 2016 11:50 AM

 Donald J. Trump ✓
@realDonaldTrump

I gave millions of dollars to DJT Foundation, raised or
recieved millions more, ALL of which is given to charity,
and media won't report!

Dec 26, 2016 9:53 PM

Donald J. Trump ✔
@realDonaldTrump

The United Nations has such great potential but right now it is just a club for people to get together, talk and have a good time. So sad!

Dec 26, 2016 4:41 PM

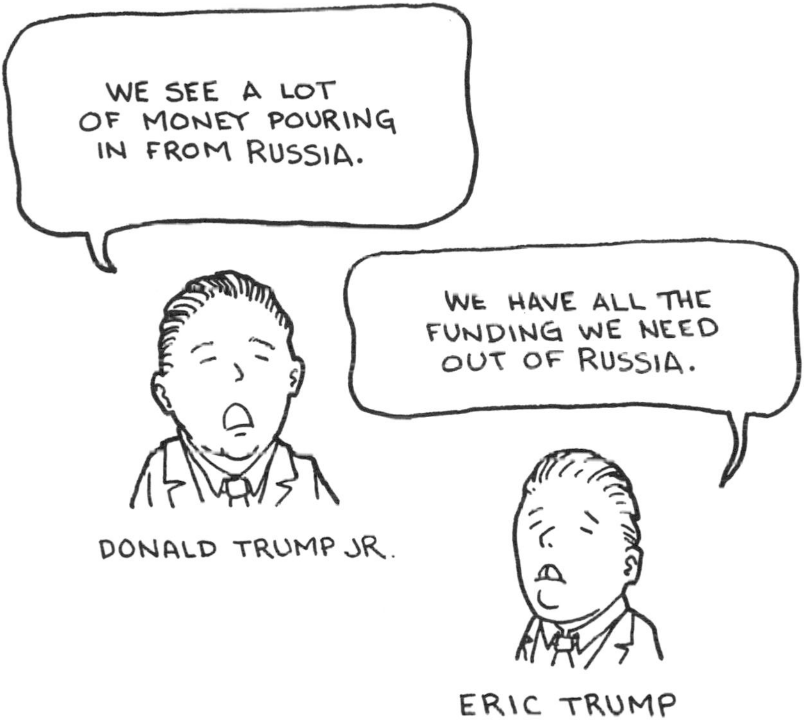
WE SEE A LOT OF MONEY POURING IN FROM RUSSIA.
DONALD TRUMP JR.
WE HAVE ALL THE FUNDING WE NEED OUT OF RUSSIA.
ERIC TRUMP

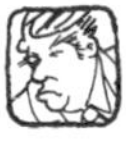

Donald J. Trump
@realDonaldTrump

Russia has never tried to use leverage over me. I HAVE NOTHING TO DO WITH RUSSIA - NO DEALS, NO LOANS, NO NOTHING!

Jan 11, 2017 7:31 AM

 **Donald J. Trump** ✔
@realDonaldTrump

The Democrats, lead by head clown Chuck Schumer, know how bad ObamaCare is and what a mess they are in. Instead of working to fix it, they..

Jan 5, 2017 6:57 AM

 Donald J. Trump ✔
@realDonaldTrump

...do the typical political thing and BLAME. The fact is ObamaCare was a lie from the beginning."Keep you doctor, keep your plan!" It is....

Jan 5, 2017 7:01 AM

 **Donald J. Trump** ✔
@realDonaldTrump

...time for Republicans & Democrats to get together and come up with a healthcare plan that really works - much less expensive & FAR BETTER!

Jan 5, 2017 7:06 AM

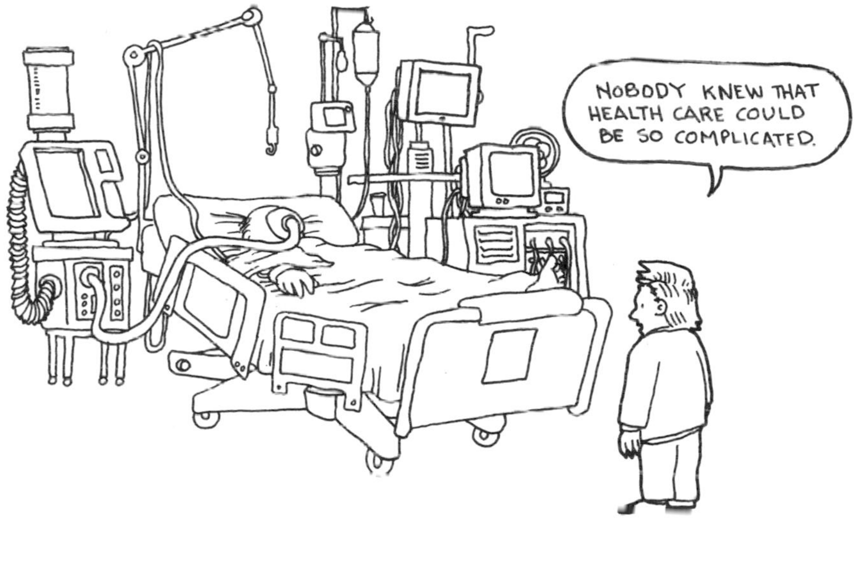
NOBODY KNEW THAT HEALTH CARE COULD BE SO COMPLICATED.

Donald J. Trump ✓
@realDonaldTrump

Intelligence agencies should never have allowed this fake news to "leak" into the public. One last shot at me.Are we living in Nazi Germany?

Jan 11, 2017 7:48 AM

 Donald J. Trump ✔
@realDonaldTrump

Congressman John Lewis should spend more time on
fixing and helping his district, which is in horrible shape
and falling apart (not to......

Jan 14, 2017 7:50 AM

 **Donald J. Trump** ✔
@realDonaldTrump

mention crime infested) rather than falsely complaining
about the election results. All talk, talk, talk – no action
or results. Sad!

Jan 14, 2017 8:07 AM

Donald J. Trump ✔
@realDonaldTrump

The "Unaffordable" Care Act will soon be history!

Jan 13, 2017 6:33 AM

 Donald J. Trump ✔
@realDonaldTrump

INTELLIGENCE INSIDERS NOW CLAIM THE TRUMP
DOSSIER IS "A COMPLETE FRAUD!" @OANN

Jan 14, 2017 8:14 AM

 **Donald J. Trump** ✓
@realDonaldTrump

Join me at 4pm over at the Lincoln Memorial with my
family! #Inauguration2017

Jan 19, 2017 3:21 PM

 Donald J. Trump ✔
@realDonaldTrump

Writing my inaugural address at the Winter White House, Mar-a-Lago, three weeks ago. Looking forward to Friday. #Inauguration

Jan 18, 2017 12:33 PM

2009 OBAMA INAUGURATION
2017 TRUMP INAUGURATION

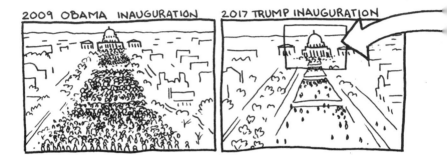

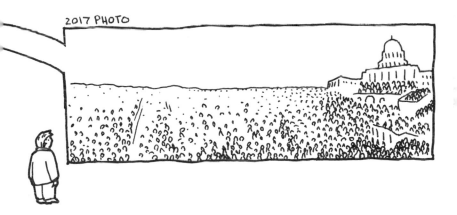

2017 PHOTO

 Donald J. Trump ✔
@realDonaldTrump

A photo delivered yesterday that will be displayed in the
upper/lower press hall. Thank you Abbas!

Jan 24, 2017 11:58 AM

 **Donald J. Trump** ✔
@realDonaldTrump

Signing orders to move forward with the construction of the Keystone XL and Dakota Access pipelines in the Oval Office.

Jan 24, 2017 12:49 PM

 Donald J. Trump ✔
@realDonaldTrump

If Chicago doesn't fix the horrible "carnage" going on,
228 shootings in 2017 with 42 killings (up 24% from
2016), I will send in the Feds!

Jan 24, 2017 9:25 PM

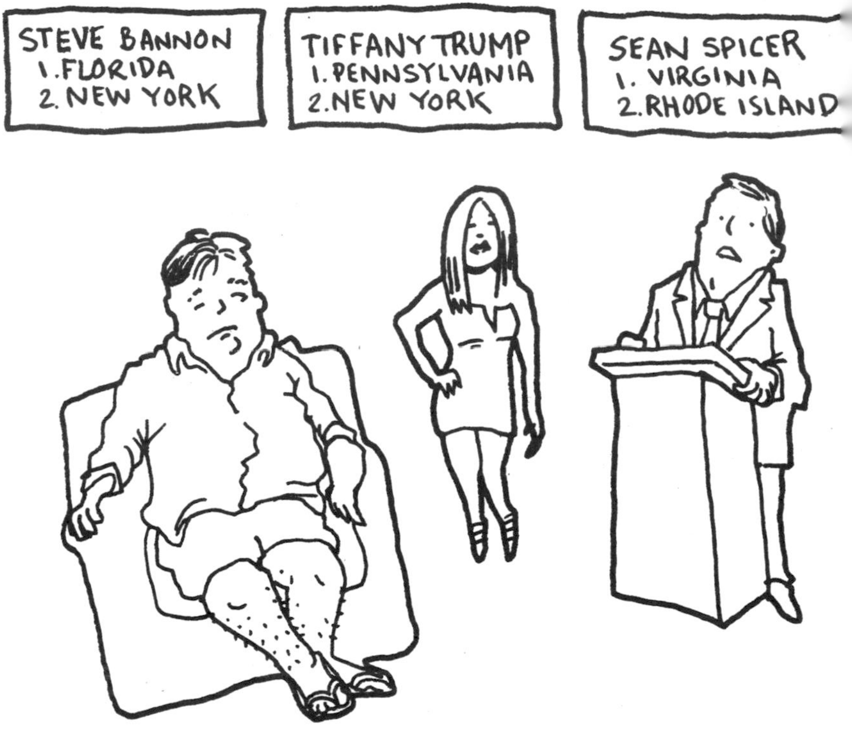
STEVE BANNON
1. FLORIDA
2. NEW YORK
TIFFANY TRUMP
1. PENNSYLVANIA
2. NEW YORK
SEAN SPICER
1. VIRGINIA
2. RHODE ISLAND

JARED KUSHNER
1. NEW YORK
2. NEW JERSEY

STEVEN MNUCHIN
1. NEW YORK
2. CALIFORNIA

 Donald J. Trump ✓
@realDonaldTrump

I will be asking for a major investigation into VOTER
FRAUD, including those registered to vote in two states,
those who are illegal and....

Jan 25, 2017 7:10 AM

 Donald J. Trump ✔
@realDonaldTrump

even, those registered to vote who are dead (and many for a long time). Depending on results, we will strengthen up voting procedures!

Jan 25, 2017 7:13 AM

Donald J. Trump ✔
@realDonaldTrump

The #MarchForLife is so important. To all of you
marching --- you have my full support!

Jan 27, 2017 11:27 AM

Donald J. Trump ✔
@realDonaldTrump

Statement on International Holocaust Remembrance
Day: whitehouse.gov/the-press-offi...

Jan 27, 2017 3:20 PM

"In the name of the perished, I pledge to
do everything in my power throughout my
Presidency, and my life, to ensure that the
forces of evil never again defeat the powers of
good. Together, we will make love and tolerance
prevalent throughout the world."

 **Donald J. Trump** ✔
@realDonaldTrump

Professional anarchists, thugs and paid protesters are proving the point of the millions of people who voted to MAKE AMERICA GREAT AGAIN!

Feb 3, 2017 6:48 AM

 **Donald J. Trump** ✔
@realDonaldTrump

We must keep "evil" out of our country!

Feb 3, 2017 6:08 PM

 Donald J. Trump ✔
@realDonaldTrump

Just cannot believe a judge would put our country in such peril. If something happens blame him and court system. People pouring in. Bad!

Feb 5, 2017 3:39 PM

 Donald J. Trump ✔
@realDonaldTrump

The judge opens up our country to potential terrorists
and others that do not have our best interests at heart.
Bad people are very happy!

Feb 4, 2017 7:48 PM

 **Donald J. Trump** ✔
@realDonaldTrump

The failing @nytimes writes total fiction concerning me.
They have gotten it wrong for two years, and now are
making up stories & sources!

Feb 6, 2017 11:32 AM

 **Donald J. Trump** ✔
@realDonaldTrump

The failing @nytimes was forced to apologize to its
subscribers for the poor reporting it did on my election
win. Now they are worse!

Feb 6, 2017 9:33 PM

 **Donald J. Trump** ✔
@realDonaldTrump

Any negative polls are fake news, just like the CNN, ABC, NBC polls in the election. Sorry, people want border security and extreme vetting.

Feb 6, 2017 7:01 AM

 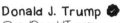 **Donald J. Trump** ✔
@realDonaldTrump

I call my own shots, largely based on an accumulation of data, and everyone knows it. Some FAKE NEWS media, in order to marginalize, lies!

Feb 6, 2017 7:07 AM

 Donald J. Trump ✔
@realDonaldTrump

It is the same Fake News Media that said there is "no path to victory for Trump" that is now pushing the phony Russia story. A total scam!

Apr 1, 2017 9:02 AM

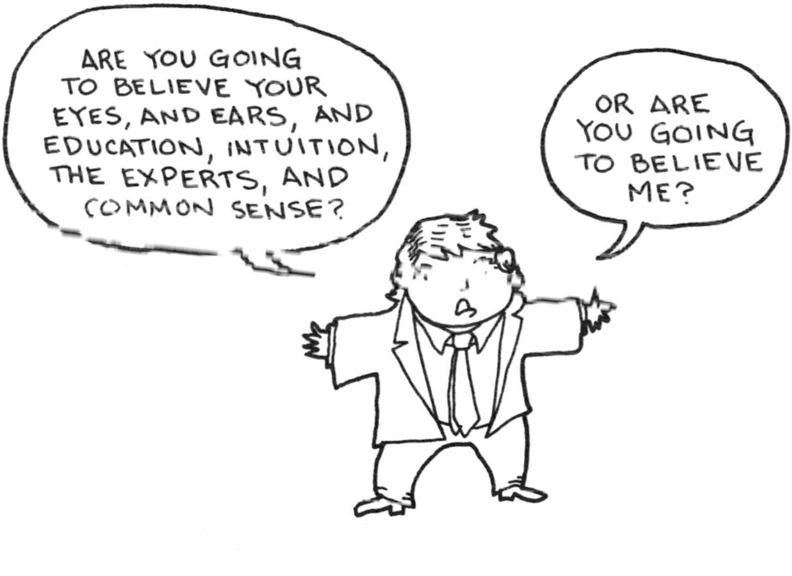
ARE YOU GOING TO BELIEVE YOUR EYES, AND EARS, AND EDUCATION, INTUITION, THE EXPERTS, AND COMMON SENSE?
OR ARE YOU GOING TO BELIEVE ME?

 **Donald J. Trump** ✔
@realDonaldTrump

SEE YOU IN COURT, THE SECURITY OF OUR NATION
IS AT STAKE!

Feb 9, 2017 6:35 PM

 Donald J. Trump ✔
@realDonaldTrump

Our legal system is broken! "77 % of refugees allowed
into U.S. since travel reprieve hail from seven suspect
countries." (WT) SO DANGEROUS!

Feb 11, 2017 7:12 AM

 **Donald J. Trump** ✔
@realDonaldTrump

My daughter Ivanka has been treated so unfairly by
@Nordstrom. She is a great person -- always pushing
me to do the right thing! Terrible!

Feb 8, 2017 10:51 AM

 Donald J. Trump ✓
@realDonaldTrump

A working dinner tonight with Prime Minister Abe of Japan, and his representatives, at the Winter White House (Mar-a-Lago). Very good talks!

Feb 11, 2017 6:24 PM

 Donald J. Trump ✓
@realDonaldTrump

The real story here is why are there so many illegal leaks coming out of Washington? Will these leaks be happening as I deal on N.Korea etc?

Feb 14, 2017 9:28 AM

Donald J. Trump ✔
@realDonaldTrump

Just leaving Florida. Big crowds of enthusiastic supporters lining the road that the FAKE NEWS media refuses to mention. Very dishonest!

Feb 12, 2017 5:19 PM

 **Donald J. Trump** ✔
@realDonaldTrump

Trump signs bill undoing Obama coal mining rule' thehill.
com/policy/energy-...

Feb 16, 2017 6:44 PM

 **Donald J. Trump** ✔
@realDonaldTrump

The FAKE NEWS media (failing @nytimes, @CNN, @NBCNews and many more) is not my enemy, it is the enemy of the American people. SICK!

Feb 17, 2017 4:32 PM

 Donald J. Trump ✔
@realDonaldTrump

"One of the most effective press conferences
I've ever seen!" says Rush Limbaugh. Many agree.
Yet FAKE MEDIA calls it differently! Dishonest

Feb 17, 2017 6:15 PM

 Donald J. Trump ✔
@realDonaldTrump

Don't believe the main stream (fake news) media.
The White House is running VERY WELL. I inherited
a MESS and am in the process of fixing it.

Feb 18, 2017 8:31 AM

 Donald J. Trump ✔
@realDonaldTrump

Very much enjoyed my tour of the Smithsonian's
National Museum of African American History and
Culture...A great job done by amazing people!

Feb 22, 2017 7:50 AM

Donald J. Trump ✔
@realDonaldTrump

Jeff Sessions is an honest man. He did not say anything wrong. He could have stated his response more accurately, but it was clearly not....

Mar 2, 2017 9:22 PM

 Donald J. Trump ✔
@realDonaldTrump

...intentional. This whole narrative is a way of saving face for Democrats losing an election that everyone thought they were supposed.....

Mar 2, 2017 9:27 PM

 **Donald J. Trump** ✔
@realDonaldTrump

...to win. The Democrats are overplaying their hand. They lost the election, and now they have lost their grip on reality. The real story...

Mar 2, 2017 9:35 PM

 Donald J. Trump ✔
@realDonaldTrump

...is all of the illegal leaks of classified and other information. It is a total `witch hunt!"

Mar 2, 2017 9:38 PM

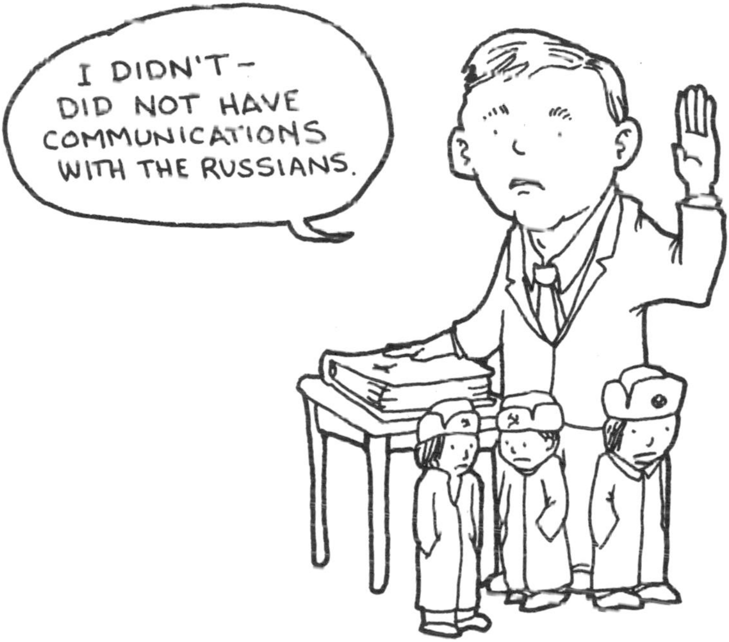
I DIDN'T - DID NOT HAVE COMMUNICATIONS WITH THE RUSSIANS.

 **Donald J. Trump** ✔
@realDonaldTrump

I will not be attending the White House Correspondents'
Association Dinner this year. Please wish everyone well
and have a great evening!

Feb 25, 2017 4:53 PM

Donald J. Trump ✔
@realDonaldTrump

Terrible! Just found out that Obama had my "wires tapped" in Trump Tower just before the victory. Nothing found. This is McCarthyism!

Mar 4, 2017 6:35 AM

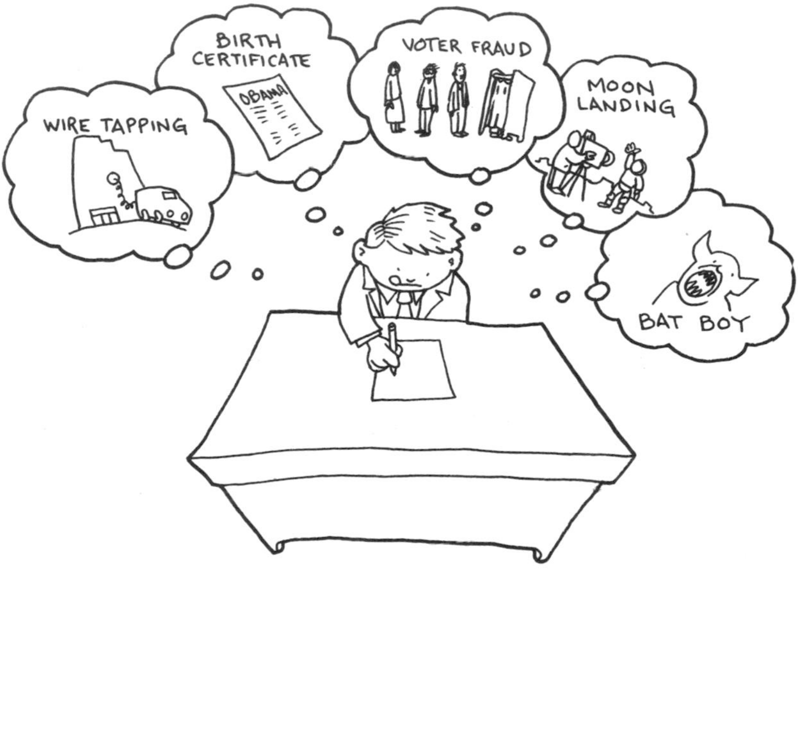
WIRE TAPPING
BIRTH CERTIFICATE
OBAMA
VOTER FRAUD
MOON LANDING
BAT BOY

 **Donald J. Trump** ✔
@realDonaldTrump

Is it legal for a sitting President to be "wire tapping" a race for president prior to an election? Turned down by court earlier. A NEW LOW!

Mar 4, 2017 6:49 AM

 Donald J. Trump ✔
@realDonaldTrump

I'd bet a good lawyer could make a great case out of the fact that President Obama was tapping my phones in October, just prior to Election!

Mar 4, 2017 6:52 AM

 Donald J. Trump ✔
@realDonaldTrump

How low has President Obama gone to tapp my phones during the very sacred election process. This is Nixon/Watergate. Bad (or sick) guy!

Mar 4, 2017 7:02 AM

 Donald J. Trump ✔
@realDonaldTrump

On International Women's Day, join me in honoring
the critical role of women here in America & around
the world.

Mar 8, 2017 6:13 AM

 Donald J. Trump ✔
@realDonaldTrump

Despite what you hear in the press, healthcare is coming along great. We are talking to many groups and it will end in a beautiful picture!

Mar 9, 2017 12:01 PM

 Donald J. Trump ✔
@realDonaldTrump

Does anybody really believe that a reporter, who nobody ever heard of, "went to his mailbox" and found my tax returns? @NBCNews FAKE NEWS!

Mar 15, 2017 6:55 AM

 Donald J. Trump 🔵
@realDonaldTrump

Thanks many are saying I'm the best 140 character writer in the world. It's easy when it's fun.

Nov 10, 2012 10:23 AM

 Donald J. Trump ✔
@realDonaldTrump

A NEW ERA IN AMERICAN ENERGY!
#MadeInTheUSA🇺🇸
Watch here: youtu.be/OdkThe_O50M

Mar 28, 2017 5:48 PM

 Donald J. Trump
@realDonaldTrump

Be prepared, there is a small chance that our
horrendous leadership could unknowingly lead us into
World War III.

Aug 31, 2013 5:46 AM

SPECIAL THANKS

Charles (@C_Brownstein) Brownstein told me to illustrate Trump's tweets in response to me complaining about doing another book of gags. He also wrote much of my introduction.

Thanks to David (@tipjar) Nicol for getting me started with thousands of Trump tweets. I also used several websites:

The Horror xbias.com/the_horror
Trump Twitter Archive www.trumptwitterarchive.com
Did Trump Tweet It? didtrumptweetit.com

Justin (@shitmydadsays) Halpern was nice enough to let me abuse his title for this book. He's funny as hell and a gentleman. Buy his other book too, *I Suck at Girls*.

Bill (@plymptoons) Plympton illustrated Kanye's tweets in *Through the Wire* long before Trump was even tweeting. I owe him a tip of the hat.

I inadvertently stole the "Asking for a Friend" gag from Andrew (@andrewaydin) Aydin, who created the amazing graphic novel trilogy *March* along with John (@repjohnlewis) Lewis and Nate (@Nate_Powell_Art) Powell.

Check out *The Unquotable Trump* by Robert (@RSikoryak) Sikoryak. He illustrates Trump quotes in various comic styles. He has a history of illustrating nonfiction and, conceptually, some of this book came from him.

Another inspiration for me is Bob (@doroughdoc) Dorough who sang a weather report, a draft card notice, a laundry ticket and more, on his album *This Is a Recording of Pop Art Songs*. Also check out his *Too Much Coffee Man* album (and *Schoolhouse Rock*).

THE TRUMP PRESIDENTIAL LIBRARY